Professional Presence How to Look, Sound and Act Like a Leader in Any Job

By Marne Platt and Cindy Steiner

Table of Contents

Chapter 1: What is Professional Presence?

Presence. It's hard to define, but we all know it when we meet someone who has it. Think of Christine Lagarde, or Dame Helen Mirren. It's not just having good posture or a strong voice and clear opinions, though these definitely contribute.

Presence comes from within. It shows in how other people perceive and react to you, your words and your actions. Professional presence is how you are perceived at work: are you seen as a leader? Do your opinions and advice carry weight? Do colleagues look to you for direction (literally or figuratively) during difficult times or awkward conversations? For people with strong professional presence, the answer to these questions is 'yes.'

Webster's online dictionary defines presence as *a*: the bearing, carriage, or air of a person; *especially*: stately or distinguished bearing or *b*: a noteworthy quality of poise and effectiveness

Think of presence as the way your internal self shows to the world. Your presence is not related to how tall you are or how much physical space you take up. It's about how much metaphorical space you fill. A woman with presence is seen as strong and worth listening to. A man without presence will be thought of as a 'worker bee' — if he is thought of much at all.

Presence and confidence complement one another. A woman with confidence automatically has some presence; she speaks up, shares her opinions and makes herself heard. If she doesn't tick the other boxes on appearance and body language though, her impact will be limited.

If you aren't a naturally confident person, and you follow the advice in this book, you will gain self-confidence just by knowing that you can 'play the game' of professional presence.

Either way, as you practice these skills, you will develop both confidence and the presence that goes with it. Soon you will be one of the people who can bring a room, a meeting, or a decision to life!

Your presence at work can be different than your presence outside of it. Think of the stereotypical overbearing boss who is a henpecked husband at home, or the accountant who is quiet and introverted in the office but runs her Community Board with strength and flair. Once you develop your presence, you can choose where and how to let your light shine!

Different factors affect your personal and professional presence:

- Body Language
- Speech
- Appearance

This book shares the secrets to building your presence through all of these, and provides simple yet ingenious small actions you can take to amplify your presence in a variety of situations.

We devote one chapter each to body language, speech and appearance. We share the powerful 'PREP' tool, and give you practice examples with suggested solutions, so you can hone your skills. Work through this book to improve your presence and have more impact in life and work.

Chapter 2: Does Your Body Language Build Your Presence or Bury It?

Everyone you know, at work or in another part of life, has an impression of you. They think of you as strong, confident, flexible, easy to talk with, intimidating, capable, unskilled, shy, friendly or even strange! That impression starts with the first time they hear anything about you and continues throughout your entire relationship -even long after you stop interacting regularly.

First impressions happen in seconds - long before you open your mouth to speak. And each time you communicate with someone, whether in person, in writing, or via indirect means like LinkedIn postings, you build their image of you. Even someone else's description of you, your work, or your activities is factored in. In this chapter, we are going to look at one of critical factors in building that impression: Body language.

Body language is one of the most important factors in determining first impressions, and how that impression changes over time. So managing your body language is one important way of managing your professional presence. In this book, we break it down into 3 basic areas:

- Posture and expression
- Eye contact
- Handshakes and gestures

Posture and Expression.

Stand up, put down this book, and walk across the room. Then come back and keep reading.

Do you stand and walk with an air of confidence? Is your head up, eyes straight ahead? Are your shoulders back? Do you have a small, confident smile?

Or do you walk with your eyes down, shoulders rounded, and a distracted or worried expression?

While both postures make a strong impression, the first posture gives an impression of confidence, the second of uncertainty. Which impression do you want to give?

Some of this is simple biology.

When you breathe while standing straight, more air gets into your lungs, so more oxygen can get to your body and brain. That helps your brain think more clearly and gives you more energy.

With your shoulders and spine hunched, you can't breathe freely. Your voice will be quieter with less air behind it, and you cut yourself off from the energy surge that comes with oxygen from deep breaths.

Posture exercise

Try this exercise now and you will see the difference. Start by standing up.

First, the 'low-presence' position. Look towards the ground, about 3 feet (1 meter) in front of you. That tilts your head down. Let your shoulders follow your head – let them curl forward a bit. Now try to take a deep breath. Try introducing yourself to an imaginary colleague. It's quite difficult to do this in a loud, confident voice.

Now, try the 'high-presence' position. Look straight ahead, at a point about 3 feet (1 meter) ahead. Bring your shoulders back, chin up and chest open.

Now try to take a deep breath and introduce yourself again to that imaginary colleague.

Do you feel the difference? In the high-presence position, you can speak more clearly, and you look other people in the eye, like an equal. In the low-presence position, you cannot physically speak in the same way, and you can't see the face of the person you are talking with, let alone look into their eyes.

Stand up straight, look your colleagues in the eye and breathe deeply. You deserve their respect and attention!

Now consider your expression. Your expression signals to the people around you whether you feel in control. If you have ever heard, thought, or said 'Stephen doesn't look happy today, I guess things really aren't going well around here' you know exactly what we mean. And it starts from the moment other people see you.

A slight smile shows that you are relaxed and confident, and on top of the moment's challenges. When you smile at someone, you let them know that you are interested in what they have to say and are engaged in the discussion.

That doesn't mean approaching every person with a wide, fake grin ('the used car salesman smile'). Some situations and some people call for a more serious expression; always be appropriate.

Eye Contact

Direct eye contact links with your expression to build your presence and signal strength and confidence. In Western cultures, strong, direct eye contact shows confidence, conviction and even honesty. For example, in the US there are expressions like "she is shifty-eyed" (don't trust this person), and "look them in the eye" (to show that you mean what you say). Looking down and avoiding eye contact give the impression that you are weak and have nothing important to say. It might even signal that you are not telling the truth! Police investigators look for lies when the person they are interviewing looks down or away from them. You certainly don't want to give that impression!

Handshakes and Gestures

All of your gestures are important, but the handshake is probably the most important, at least in the West. We will start with the handshake, and then move on to more general comments about your gestures.

In the West, the handshake is the normal business greeting. A person with a strong handshake firmly clasps the other person's hand, pumps up and down once, twice, or a maximum of 3 times, and then releases the other hand without dropping it - all while looking into the other person's eyes.

Sounds easy, right? Well, not really. Many people, both men and women with weak handshakes use either the 'Sleeping Beauty' or the 'Secret Princess' approach. Each gives a weak impression.

In the Sleeping Beauty handshake, their hand is limp and unmoving. The person they are supposed to be greeting as an equal has to do all the work to make the handshake.

This gives the impression that they are either not interested in the discussion, or not able to interact as an equal.

With the 'Secret Princess' handshake, the person's hand half-clasps their handshake partner's. Only the fingertips are involved, as if he or she is waiting for a prince to lift and kiss it. Trust me, this is not going to happen in business!

If you use the Sleeping Beauty or Secret Princess, you probably look down at your linked hands while doing it. When you shake hands this way, you signal weakness or subservience. Is that what you want to project?

Of course not! Practice your handshake until it is strong and confident, and you can do it while maintaining eye contact with the other person.

After the handshakes are done, your other gestures are still important. Do you wave your hands around, beyond the range of your body? That can signal passion, or lack of self-control. Do it selectively. Think of orchestral conductors: they change the flamboyance of their gestures to reflect the music's volume and tempo. In the same way, your gestures should accentuate your speech, not overwhelm it.

Many of us have physical tics, too. These are unconscious gestures we make whenever we are nervous or uncomfortable. They distract from your presence by distracting others from your message. People are too busy watching you twist your hair or tap your fingers to really pay attention. Other common physical tics include tapping a toe, clicking a pen, cracking your knuckles, or shifting your weight from one leg to the other. Some of them annoy your colleagues, others give the impression that you need to use the bathroom! All signal that you are not 100% in control of yourself, and that undermines your presence.

Learning to walk, make eye contact, shake hands and gesture appropriately all improve the unspoken impression you make on those around you. They signal confidence, self-control and comfort, even in tricky situations. All of these build your professional presence. They are equally important when giving presentations, sitting in a meeting, or standing at the coffee machine. Practice until you master them. When you do, you will be able to walk into your next meeting with your head up, make eye contact, and give the other person a firm handshake while smiling confidently. They will automatically know that you have a lot to contribute!

Chapter 3: Speak Like a Professional – Declare your presence when you speak

Meet Julie and William, two marketing professionals working on 2 different new promotional campaigns. Today they are presenting competing funding requests to the board of directors. Both have worked on their projects for months and are sure they are ready for the next steps. Board members are familiar with both projects. We'll step in during the closing moments of each presentation.

> *William*: So, you can see, this idea is awesome! Customers will love it, and we need to be on the market really soon. I only need like $75,000 to get to launch. That's not much when you think about what we can get back. Can I go forward?

Julie: A $75,000 investment lets us launch in 6 months. I project 20% market share in the first year, for topline sales of $750,000. With a 35% gross margin, that means over $250,000 in profit next year. Do you confirm the investment?

Two different ways of asking for the same amount of money. Which request would you approve?

When you speak in business, your words only make up part of the message. Your tone of voice, the words you use (and how you use them), even how quickly you handle interruptions contribute to the overall impression.

In this section we review factors that can make your speaking style fit workplace expectations, so you sound believable and reliable. We will also introduce a powerful tool, the PREP model, that will make you more convincing. As more of your requests are approved, your reputation, confidence and presence will grow.

Tone

Everyone has a natural tone of voice. For some it's deep (think of the 1970s soul singer Barry White). For others, it's light and breathy (think of Marilyn Monroe). Most of us fall somewhere in between. While a deep voice, or one that carries naturally through a crowd can instantly add presence, anyone can use these tips to make their voice more effective in the workplace.

Be natural Be yourself. Trying to sound like someone else is like lip-synching on stage: eventually you are caught and look foolish.

Let your voice rise and fall, get louder or softer, naturally depending on the content of your message.

Keep your tone even Speak at a steady pace and in a moderate pitch without being monotonous. When you talk for a long time, or repeat something you have said many times before, it's easy to drone on. You might not even have to think about what you are saying. That's a sure way to turn off your listeners! They don't like listening to monotonous speakers any more than you do. Stay steady, stay confident, and stay interesting.

Avoid Uptalk Uptalk is the unconscious habit of ending sentences on a higher note. It turns every statement into a question, and makes you sound tentative and insecure. That certainly won't build a strong presence! While uptalk is often considered a female tendency, I have cringed at enough men uptalking on podcasts to realize that it is a gender-neutral problem.

Sound like an adult if you have adopted the "Mini Mouse/Helpless Little Girl (or Boy) Voice" get a voice coach! This high-pitched, breathy tone makes you sound like a 5-year old, not a confident professional. Using the Mini Mouse voice not only undermines your presence, it can even cost you promotions. No business wants executives who sound like they have just come off the playground. You are an adult; sound like one.

Word selection

We all know that every word matters in public speaking. And the words you choose for a presentation or speech certainly deserve close attention. But to reinforce the strong professional presence you want to build, you need to pay attention to the words you use in everyday discussions, too.

The exact words you choose matter. Speak in a language that the other person understands. That means avoiding jargon and abbreviations, especially if it is only to show off your knowledge. Don't say you want to socialize a proposal; say you plan to discuss it with the heads of sales and manufacturing.

Sometimes words creep into our speech unrecognized. We repeat them over and over until they become fillers, sort of a verbal tic to fill time. They don't support the message, they distract your listener, and they make you sound unsure. None of these will strengthen your professional presence!

Common fillers include:

Actually	In other words	That is to say
To make a long story short	Clearly	Well
In reality	Literally	Like
Um/uh	Thus	You know
Of course	Basically	I think/I guess

Have these killer fillers crept into your speech? If so, you need to kick them out!

Exercise: Ditching the Killer Fillers
If you struggle with fillers, try this exercise.

First, track your use of fillers for one week. You can try to do it yourself or ask a colleague for help. Keep track of which words you use, in what situations, and how many times. Some people have more than one -even as many as 4 or5! At the end of the week, pick your Killer Filler word.

For the next few weeks, keep track only of how many times you say that one word. Each week, work on reducing that number by at least 10%. If you say the word 50 times in one week, the next week try limiting it to no more than 45 times. Keep repeating this every week and soon you will have removed this Killer Filler from your repertoire!

Speaking in the active tense is another important part of word selection. Think back to grammar classes when you were a child. The active tense is where all the action is. In the passive tense, no one does anything. All the world's actions just happen by luck or magic. Decisions are taken, mistakes are made, goals are reached – but no one did anything to make that happen!

Do you really want to give away credit for your accomplishments like that? Of course not!

When you use the active tense, you take ownership of your decisions and actions. That's powerful! It's even more powerful in business because it is so rare. If you chose to take a risk, say 'I decided.' Don't distance yourself from it by saying 'A decision was taken.' Even if that risk didn't work out, show that you are dealing with it. Say 'I decided to launch the campaign. It didn't generate the sales we expected, so now we are doing XYZ and I anticipate that sales will grow even more.'

The active voice is always more concise than the passive voice. Converting to active tense automatically removes the 'to be' conjugation, saving words. Eliminating fillers is also easier in the active tense, because you engage with the action behind the words.

There's a great power in words, if you don't hitch too many of them together

Josh Billings, American Humorist

How can you check for the active vs. passive tense? Listen for the first verb in your sentences. Listen for are, were, will be, or was, followed by another verb in the past, like 'was decided' or 'will be considered' – these signal the passive tense. If your verbs are action words, like 'launched' 'closed' or 'sold,' congratulations! the active tense is your home. Taking responsibility for your actions shows self-confidence and builds presence.

Similarly, own what you don't know. A strong presence does not mean that you have all the answers. It means that you have the confidence to handle the questions. If someone asks you a tough question, consider your answer before responding. Admit if you don't know the answer and commit to finding out what it is.

Let's check in with William and Julie again. It's one year later, and things haven't gone according to plan for either of them. Julie received her funding right away, but sales are not meeting her projections. William received his funding 3 months later, after some intense coaching and back-room support from his manager. In the meantime, a competitor launched a similar product and the customers bought that instead. They are now both in front of the management board, explaining their results.

> *William*: Um well, the decision to fund this product unfortunately was not made for like 3 months. In the meantime, a

competing product was launched by our biggest competitor and customers actually liked it too. So to catch up, a decision needs to be made to put more resources behind our launch; another $75,000 should do it, OK?

Julie: We successfully launched our new product as planned. Although we have not seen quite the market share I expected, customers are still interested, and we have $400,000 in sales already. Purchasers love how easy the product is to use. Working with our sales team, I developed a new campaign, rewarding new purchasers with extra technical support and points in our very successful loyalty program. It will close the gap to my initial projections within 6 months. If you approve an additional $25,000 spend for loyalty points today I can close that gap within 3 months. Our product meets our customers' needs and sales are growing. Do you confirm the investment?

Look for the differences: William sounds far less confident than Julie. He uses fillers and the passive tense. Julie acknowledges her responsibility and emphasizes her corrective actions and what they will deliver, avoiding Killer Fillers and staying in the active tense. Once again, management granted Julie's request but not William's.

Interruptions

At some point in your career, whether you are presenting or speaking one-on-one, someone will interrupt you. How you react to that interruption speaks volumes about your confidence, and thus affects the way people see your presence.

People interrupt for many reasons: they disagree with the statement, they want to correct a mistake, they are tired of listening to you, or they don't respect your right to speak. At the bottom, it doesn't matter why they interrupt you. What matters is how you respond.

Your response depends on the circumstances and content of the interruption. Certainly, if you have misspoken about a fact, you can thank the person for pointing it out, reinforce the correction and go on. Someone who speaks over you because they don't respect your right to speak needs to be put in their place, immediately and with grace.

Consistent points to use:

Stay calm An interruption is no different from a question, in that your ability to respond calmly dictates your success and affects your reputation and presence.

Use standard responses Prepare some standard language that you can comfortably say while under pressure. Remove the pressure of having to think of a good rejoinder in the moment.

Use thanks appropriately Thank someone who makes a valid point. If it's a simple correction of a misstatement, thank them and move on. If it's valid but you aren't yet finished, thank them for the point and tell them that you will be interested in hearing more when you have finished speaking.

Maintain your authority Some people just want to hear themselves speak, or be the center of attention. As a presenter, you own the room and the right to be heard. If you are still building your presence and reputation, people might think they can just speak over you without consequences. Depending on how often that happens, and whether their content is relevant, use another version of the statement you use with someone making a valid point. Thank them for their thoughts and remind them that they will have the chance to respond when you have finished.

Be self-aware Check whether you really should stop talking. Don't monopolize a conversation. That's poor manners and a bad strategy overall. If you really have been going on for 20 minutes in what is supposed to be a dialogue, stop talking!

Business communications have a purpose, and that purpose is usually convincing someone of something. In this section, you will learn a powerful tool to create strong, concise arguments and increase your chances of getting the answer you want. Like all good tools, it's simple and powerful. It's called PREP.

PREP stands for **P**osition – **R**eason – **E**xample – **P**osition. First state your position, or what you want your listener to do, then tell them why, give an example that supports your reasoning, and restate your position or request.

For example: Imagine that you are a member of a Swiss trade delegation, visiting food company executives in another country to try to increase sales of Swiss chocolate. Your PREP might look like this:

Position: Tell them what you want them to do/believe/understand. (You should only buy Swiss chocolate)

Reason: Tell them why they should believe you. (It's the best tasting and highest quality chocolate)

Example(s) or Brief Explanation: Give 2 or 3 facts to back up your statement. (Swiss chocolatiers use only the best quality cocoa and milk from Swiss cows. They blend it according to time-tested recipes, and get it to stores quickly so you can enjoy a fresh treat).

Position: Repeat your original position with a call to action. (Why eat anything but the best? Import more delicious Swiss chocolate now)

PREP fits almost any proposal. Asking for a job? Tell them why they should hire you. Need to fund a project? State what you need and what you will deliver with it (look at Julie's proposal at the beginning of this chapter for an example of using PREP for requesting funding. Elegant, isn't it?).

Try it for yourself now. Imagine yourself asking yor manager to fund your next project, like Julie and William. What do you need? Why should they give it to you? How will you present your rationale?

The secret to great PREPping is to practice, practice, practice until your PREP is short (less than 1 minute), focused on what interests your listeners, and feels natural to you. Start by writing out the 4 steps, then practice them out loud until you like what you hear. Practice in front of a mirror, on video or with a trusted friend.

Appendix 1 of this book is a PREP worksheet that will help you organize your thoughts. Download it for free at www.fundamentalcapabilities.com or www.steinerinternational.com

Appendix 2 of this book gives you some more PREP practice scenarios with suggested solutions.

PREPping helps you build concise, effective proposals with a higher likelihood of success. One executive uses PREP as a filter that prevents him from using any weak argument that comes to mind. PREP forces him to think about his strongest points, refine his key messages, and present a well-thought out request. Using PREP builds confidence, and as your confidence grows, so does your presence.

Once you are comfortable with PREP, you can move into advanced versions. See our PREP workbook *'Prepping For Success: How to Position Yourself and Your Requests to Get the Answers You Need'* for how and when to lead with the reasons (RPEP) or leave the reason out entirely (PEP)

Chapter 4: Appearance: How You Look is Who You Are

You have your own unique style and look. It reflects your personality, your preferences, and, directly or indirectly, your status. At work, it can signal your position in the hierarchy. Look around your office. Do all of the senior executives, male and female, wear grey suits? Or do they wear the casual version of the uniform, khaki trousers and a polo top? The clothes you choose can signal how much respect you deserve.

Fair or not, how you look is who you are. Your choice of clothes, shoes and accessories signal your credibility, professionalism and trustworthiness, long before you speak. For women, this includes your handbag, your makeup and your jewelry. For men, it includes ties, belt buckles and jewelry. What does your work attire say about you?

This is not a book on style, or on selecting clothes that fit your body type. Many resources exist to help you do that, from personal shoppers to books, websites and apps. This chapter looks at your wardrobe in relation to building your presence. Whether you are male or female, most of the same strategies will work.

Keeping that in mind, let's look at how your appearance impacts your presence, and what you can do to influence it.

What to Wear

In almost any industry profession, or social group, broader societal norms still apply. Distractingly deep necklines on men or women, miniskirts, no socks, piercing and tattoos generally work to undermine a professional presence (rock stars and artists excepted, of course).

Geography influences work attire too. The California dress code is more relaxed than that of Boston (think Google vs. Boston Consulting). In international business Americans are often expected to be less formal than Japanese executives. Dressing too informally can backfire, so be sure to calibrate your professional look with your town, industry, company and function.

Dress for your body type
Choose clothing that fits your body type. Women can be rectangles, pears, apples or hourglasses. Men can be rectangles, triangles (right side up or inverted), ovals or rhomboids. Regardless of how much you weigh, unless you

are truly obese, your shape will show. Each shape looks better in a different clothing style.

For example:

So-called "pear-shaped' women look best with clothes that help balance their larger lower halves by drawing the eye upward, like V-necks or statement necklaces. Women with more rectangular shapes may want to add curves by, for example, adding a belt to emphasize their waists. Men with a more generous middle look far better in single-breasted suits and shirts with subtle vertical striping. Double-breasted suits will only add more bulk. Have that super-fit inverted triangle shape? Avoid padded shoulders or you will look like the Incredible Hulk.

If you aren't sure of your shape, look for advice online, in books or from advisors in stores. You can even bring a friend to the store with you. Choose clothes that emphasize your best features. You will feel more confident and look more professional: two ways to build your presence.

Work environment

Choose an outfit that matches the norms for your profession and your company. Brightly coloured, stylish clothes won't work in a conservative profession like the law, but they could be perfect in a tech startup. The same applies to accessories: look for pieces that pull a look together without overwhelming it. Make sure that whatever you wear is appropriate to the situation of the day.

The environment can even change from job to job within the same company. For example, one of us (Marne) worked for many years in the pharmaceutical industry. It's conservative and old-fashioned where style is concerned – unless you are in manufacturing or a laboratory, where it is much more casual. In senior management roles and roles that involved talking with government agencies and doctors, a dark suit with conservative heels and strong, subtle jewelry was absolutely required. In manufacturing, the same outfit was just too much. It even got in the way of doing the job, because colleagues found it unapproachable. Neat jeans or khaki trousers and polo shirts fit much better, and encouraged the debate and exchange that were absolutely essential for solving problems in this environment.

Comfort

Work days are long, and you may find yourself standing or sitting in the same position for hours. If you're clothes aren't comfortable, you will suffer, squirm, and be distracted. That's a sure way to undermine your presence. Keep this in mind when building your wardrobe. This is not the time for 'wishful' pants (those you wished that you didn't fill quite so much). Nor is it the place for shoes that don't quite fit, rings that slip, or shirts that won't stay tucked in. Make sure that you can move freely in your clothes, without feeling any pinching or binding.

If you travel often, look for clothes that can make the trip with you. One secret to looking great while traveling is to pick a colour family for the trip – perhaps blues or greys – and bring an assortment of clothes to mix and match. Choose fabrics that resist wrinkling, can hide the occasional small spot or stain, and wash clean easily. Most of us have had to wash a shirt in the hotel sink at some point. Knowing that the stain will come out, and that we will still look presentable in the morning, is priceless!

Use accessories wisely

If you're wearing quality basics, people notice your accessories more. Use them to add personality, change your look, and give a nod to fashion. You can sometimes save money here: no need to spend your entire clothing budget on a genuine hand-dyed silk scarf when there are plenty of beautiful acrylic ones to be had.

Accessories for Women	Accessories for Men
Scarves or shawls for warmth and style	Brighter ties
Handbag or computer bag	Computer bag
Rings, earrings, pins and necklaces: understated vs.	Phone case

statement pieces	
Phone case	Rings
Watch	Pastel shirt or subtle print shirt
	French cuffs and cufflinks
	Watch

Use bright colours and patterns to liven up your basic suits and khakis.

Like accessories, your hair and makeup contribute to your overall look and deserve your attention. Haircut fashion changes all the time (remember side parts? Or the quiff?), as does the fashion in makeup. Regardless of what's hot right now, certain styles or colours will fit your face's structure or your skin tones best. If you aren't sure of what will work for you, consult an expert. Ask a colleague whose hair you admire for their stylist's or colourist's name. For makeup advice, consult a specialist in one of the better stores. Look for tips online and try some of them on at home or with friends before wearing them to work. On a budget? Hunt on line for product reviews. You might be surprised - one of the least expensive mascaras, from Maybelline, consistently gets higher reviews than more expensive competitors. To save money on haircuts, splurge on a fancy stylist once or twice to get the cut you want, then keep it neat for several months at a less expensive salon. Whatever route you take, choose hair and makeup that make you feel 'put together' and are easy to maintain yourself. You will feel more confident, and that will translate directly to greater presence.

Use your professional clothing budget wisely

Give yourself a budget for your work clothes. Pick a number that you can afford, and then make the most of it. Shop the sales, explore commission shops. Buy the best that you can afford at the time and look for high quality pieces. In fact, you are better off with fewer high-quality items that will last for several seasons, than with many low-quality items that fall apart the first time you wash them and have to be replaced.

Invest in the important basics and take care of them. Deal with stains immediately, wash your clothes in the gentle cycle, polish your shoes and maintain the heels and soles.

The Basics for Women	The Basics for Men
Black and/or navy blue trousers -2 pair	Dark blue suit with moderate lapels
Black and/or navy blue blazer	Grey suit with moderate lapels
Classic button-down shirts in colours that complement your skin and hair tones	Classic button-down shirts in white, muted pinstripes or pale colours
Well-fitting, pressed khakis	Well-fitting, pressed khakis
Collared shirts	Collared shirts

| Black pumps with a solid, medium heel | Traditional solid-colour tie |
| Black flats or closed shoes with a professional appearance | Black lace-up or slip on business shoes |

Remember your clothing foundations too: bras and underwear for women, underwear for men, socks for everyone. Even a designer suit will suffer if these small items are ragged or don't fit well.

Chapter 5: Subtle tricks to build presence

Presence is greater than the sum of its parts. It's more than your handshake, your attire or the words you use. Remember the Webster's definition: it's the bearing, carriage, or air of a person. How do you reinforce it, to reach that subtle and powerful level of noteworthy poise and effectiveness?

This chapter includes a range of tips and tricks. Some are subtle, some not. All will help you increase your professional presence.

General meeting tips

These days, most of us spend our time in meetings, whether large or small, in person or virtual. Even before the meeting starts, your behavior signals your status, and can add to or detract from your presence. For example:

Accepting or declining invitations You do not have to attend every meeting to which you are invited! Meetings detract from working time. If the meeting doesn't require your specific attendance, either to contribute, to learn something, or to make a decision, consider declining. At least consider attending only part of the meeting. Discuss that with the organizer first, so she is not surprised, and present it as wanting to focus your attention where it is needed most. Then engage completely in the portions you do attend. If you do decline a meeting, you don't need to give explanations. A simple 'Sorry, I am not available then' suffices. For important meetings, consider offering an alternative that fits your schedule.

Greeting attendees As we will see in the section on making small talk, many people are reluctant to start a conversation with people they don't know. Introducing yourself to people you haven't met is an easy conversation starter. Be careful though; if someone asks you for a coffee, either tell them where they can get it for themselves or who can get it for them. don't let yourself be relegated to the role of 'meeting Mommy.'

Opening the conference line depending on your level of confidence and technical abilities, you can either open the line yourself, showing that you are in charge of the agenda and have mastered the phone system, or you can ask someone to do it. Understand your company's norms and follow them.

Calling the meeting to order Have you ever been in a meeting where 1 person starts to speak and everyone else quiets down? That person is often the one with the most presence, and that's who you want to be. A simple phrase like 'let's get started' is enough to signal that the time for chit-chat has ended. Move into the agenda and get going.

Choose your seat carefully

Your seat selection signals how much power you have to other attendees. It can influence how strongly your opinion is considered and whether you are even heard. People with a strong presence tend naturally to take influential seats, no matter what the table arrangements are. Which seats do they look for? That depends on the setup and the meeting purpose.

Where a final decision is needed, the head of the table, with the back to the window, is usually the most powerful seat (the dark seat in the diagram below). Notice how many times the senior person or meeting chair sits there. People whose input the decider values most usually sit immediately to her right or left. The farther you are from the head of the table, the less power you have. The least powerful seats are against the wall. These seats are usually taken by junior associates supporting their managers with details, or those allowed to observe but not participate. Do NOT take a seat against the wall when you deserve one at the table!

Power Seat in a Meeting Room

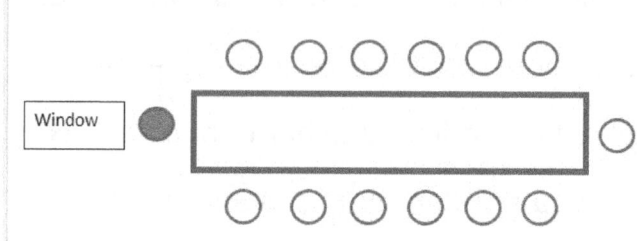

If the table is long and skinny, the center seat on each side can be the dominant seat (the 2 dark seats in the diagram below). Picture a recent news clip of a government or business negotiation; the two sides face each other across a long rectangular table. Lead negotiators for each side sit in the middle, with advisors fanning out to her sides. By sitting in the middle, the lead negotiator sends the message that she is open and ready to work together, while at the same time making it clear that on her side of the table, she is in charge. The further away from that center of power a person sits, the less influence she has in the negotiation. This is all clear before anyone says a word. Again, the least powerful seats are against the wall – so far from the power of the meeting that they are not even at the table.

Power Seats At a Long Skinny Table

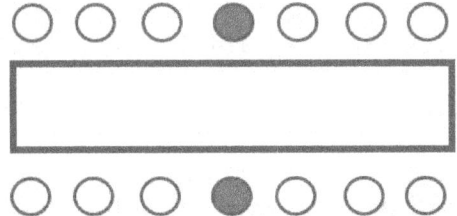

Seating can also signal openness to cooperate. In bilateral meetings (with only 2 people), place yourself to signal this. Sit next to the other person instead across the table. This signals openness to their point of view. You are in effect seeing things from their side.

Seating Arrangements for Cooperative Bilaterals

When you walk into a meeting room, where do you sit? Are you front and center, or are you in a seat that undermines your presence? Choose carefully!

The next time you walk into a meeting room, choose a seat at the main table, near the center of power. If you are the meeting chair, take the power seat. I guarantee you, if you are sitting in a powerful seat, no one will ask you to get the coffee or take the minutes. You will immediately have more credibility and influence. Try it!

Making Small Talk

We've all been there: arrived too early at a meeting, been stuck on the bathroom line at the break, or seated with strangers at a business meal or on the plane. Humans are social beings, and we want to fill the silence with conversation. We want the connections, though many of us don't know how to start. That's what small talk is for!

When other sit uncomfortably, hoping someone else will give them an opening, the person with presence is the one who breaks the ice. Doing so shows confidence, one of those foundations of presence.

How do you start a conversation with a stranger? Simple questions work best. Anyone can answer them without much thought, and you can keep the conversation going with a simple 'tell me more.' Here's a short list of icebreaker questions that you can use to get a conversation started:

- Where did you grow up? What was it like growing up there?
- What do you like to do in your spare time? How did you become involved in that?
- Who is someone you admire and would like to emulate?
- Have you traveled much? What cities/countries have you visited, and which was your favorite?
- Have you ever lived in another country?
- Do you speak any other languages?
- What did you do last weekend?
- I'm curious, what made you choose the career you did?

- Are there any particular events which you would say contributed most to your success in your career at this point?
- What advice would you give a young, upcoming colleague in your field?
- What do you think of "......"? (a current event, avoiding topics that are politically sensitive!)

Use words that you are comfortable with, and don't worry if your first question sounds forced. The person you are talking with will be grateful for any opener!

You can also explore topics like film, family, sports, and the economy. Try to avoid politics (too risky) and the weather (too boring).

Exercise: Small talk warmup
Imagine that you are on a plane, preparing for a 1 hour flight. The person sitting next to you is a stranger about whom you know nothing, except that they are reading a copy of the latest National Geographic magazine. The pilot announces a 1-hour departure delay due to weather problems between your departure and destination cities. You decide to practice your small talk skills with this person.

Select 3 small talk topics. For each, imagine a successful conversation lasting at least 10 minutes from each one. Where does the conversation lead? What questions might they ask you? Does this add any new topics to your small talk list?

Foreign languages

Working with people from other cultures can be intimidating, even for seasoned executives. It's easy to retreat into familiarity, sticking close to people who speak your language fluently. That's a lost opportunity! Learn a few words in your counterpart's language. Hello, please, thank you, yes and no are good starters. So are 'my name is ---' and I'm sorry, I don't speak ___ well.' Just making the effort shows confidence and will increase their respect for you. With respect comes (you guessed it) their perception of your presence!

Calm in a crisis

When everyone is falling apart, the leader is the one who seems to have it all, or at least some of it, together. Pull together what you have learned about words, tone, posture, gestures, expression and actions. Consciously project the impression that you can handle what life is throwing at you. If necessary, fake it till you make it. Melt down in the bathroom, if you have to, but not in public. Just being a little bit calmer and more controlled than the people around you will do wonders for your reputation – and you might even find that you are actually good in a crisis!

Chose and emulate role models

Role models, those men and women possessing the undefinable poise that signals presence, are all around you. Look for some at work and in your social groups. Look outward and find people like Christine Lagarde, Tim Cook, Christiane Amanpour, even Prince William. They all seem to be comfortable in the spotlight, even when those lights are flashing and red. Study them: how to do they talk, gesture, make eye contact, and respond to awkward questions? Use them as springboards to launch you into new behaviours.

Chapter 6: Exercises to Build Your Personal and Professional Presence

Building presence takes time and practice. Review the exercises in this book:

- Chapter 2: Posture
- Chapter 3: Handshakes
- Chapter 3: Killer Fillers
- Chapter 5: Small talk topics

Next, work through the case studies below. There are no single correct answers; create some that work for you. Find some suggested solutions in Appendix 3

Case Study 1

After 2 months of dedicated work, including evenings and weekends, you completed an in-depth analysis of your company's product mix. You have identified 3 areas to improve: product pricing, customer segmentation, and vendor selection for raw materials.

Your manager supports your conclusions and arranges for you to present your results in person to the company leadership team. These are people at least 2 levels above you, whom you have never met. At least one of them will resist your recommendations.

Answer these questions as they relate to creating a sense of presence for your presentation:

- What information will you prepare for the meeting?
- What will you wear?

- What questions can you anticipate and how will you answer them?
- The 'resisting' leader challenges the accuracy of your analysis of product pricing, saying 'you aren't from marketing, what do you know about the marketplace pricing pressure?' How do you answer?

Case Study 2

You own a shirt-making firm in a medium-sized city. A fire at your factory releases thick black smoke into the air, causing the fire department and local government to instruct people to shut their windows and stay indoors. That afternoon, as you are trying to locate all of your employees and contact your insurance company, a reporter from the local TV station arrives with film crew. His first question is 'what toxic chemicals did you have in your plant?'

- How do you respond to his questions?

- What should your demeanor (tone of voice, gestures, facial expressions) communicate?

- After the interview, your assistant asks you the same question. You know that his grandmother lives near the plant, and that they are very close. How do you respond?

Case Study 3

You are attending a networking event for your industry, given by a major company in the field. You don't know very many people, but you think this could be a great opportunity to find some customers, or even a new job.

- How do you prepare for the event?

- What do you wear?

- Do you prepare small talk topics as icebreakers? Which ones?

- One hour into the event, someone you just met, who has obviously spent too much time at the bar, begins following you and insists on joining your conversations. How do you react?

Appendix 1: PREP worksheet

The PREP Model

For Interviews, Q&A, Elevator pitch....

Analyze your audience:

1. Who are they?
2. What do they know or not know about your subject?
3. What do you want them to do?
4. Why should they care?

Then PREP: **P**osition – **R**eason – **E**xample - **P**osition

Position: Tell them what you want them to do/believe/understand. (You should only buy Swiss chocolate)

Reason: Tell them why they should believe you. (It's the best tasting and highest quality chocolate)

Example(s) or Brief Explanation: Give 2 or 3 facts to back up your statement. (Swiss chocolatiers use only the best quality cocoa and milk from Swiss cows. They blend it according to proven recipes, and get it to stores quickly so you can enjoy a fresh treat).

Position: Repeat your original position with a call to action. (Why eat anything but the best? Buy some of my delicious Swiss chocolate now)

Appendix 2: PREP Practice Scenarios

1) You have applied for a position at a highly-regarded corporation – your dream career – and are preparing for your first interview with them. You've done your homework and know all about their services, clients, and exactly what they need for this position. Use the PREP Model to create a Personal Pitch that shows that you are their BEST CHOICE! Your Personal Pitch should be no longer than one minute, so be sure to practice aloud several times with a timer before the interview.

2) You are going to a conference where you'll have lots of opportunities to network with potential clients. Use the

PREP Model to create your Personal Pitch that you can use easily and adapt to specific individuals, industries, and companies. Again, one minute is all the time you have, so practice with a timer several times beforehand.

3) You have been working on a high-stakes project for the better part of this past year and are now ready to present a proposal to the Board of Directors at your company. Keep in mind that too many details can kill it, so keep it high level and consider what's important to the Board – most likely, above all – ROI! Be over-prepared and have lots of backup data at your fingertips for the Board meeting. Use the PREP Model to create your quick "Elevator Pitch" that

you can use to pique their interest and send it via email or speak to each individual by phone before the meeting so you can get their input and anticipate questions and challenges.

4) You've been invited to a party and you know that certain individuals there have different views from you politically AND one of these individuals in particular loves to spout off about any new issue he has heard anything about. So, you know he will bring up the subject of "nationalism and its merits vs. globalism." You've known this individual for four years now and he still can't figure out where you stand politically because you have fun using the PREP Model to answer-but-not really-answer

his questions. Use the PREP Model to state your Position (which is ambiguous), give the Reason (the WHY), give Example/s, and paraphrase your Position.

These are possible answers for each of the practice scenarios. Use them as guides. Your own answers need to be true to your own situation and your own personality. Imitating someone else will not build your own personal presence.

<u>Your dream career interview personal pitch:</u>

Position: Your job description fits my expertise perfectly.

Reason: The reason I say that is I have had professional experience in all your required areas.

Example: A couple of examples – I have 15 years' experience working in the healthcare industry, which is one of your requirements. I was promoted to manage my peers two years ago, so I know how to transition from peer to manager (another of your prerequisites). And, to give you a few more examples...

Position: So, as you can see, I have the expertise to excel in this new position.

Attending a conference with lots of opportunities to network:

Position: Hello my name is ... and I'm an international executive communications coach.

Reason: I've been coached CEOs, Executive Teams, and Management level in and from several different countries for 20+ years.

Example: For example, I coach CEOs on their investor pitches, IPOs, Board meetings, and more. I also coach executives and management level on how to pitch their ideas to get results and handle challenges – be it to the Board, customers, clients, partners... And I offer leadership coaching for newly appointed managers and executives on how to best communicate with their targets, direct reports, etc.

Position: As you can see, I am a seasoned international executive communications coach able to improve peoples' performance at many levels.

Presenting your project proposal to the Board:

Position: This new service will increase our visibility, our customer base, and our profit by ≥14%.

Reason: Our customers have been asking for this new service; they desperately need it to help them store and access their data safely. Because it makes use of our existing capabilities, it's pure profit.

Example: In addition to data storage, customers need easy access to the data. They want to manage their data and access it at will. One of our biggest customers told me earlier this year that if we couldn't provide the entire package, they would have to change providers and go with our competitor. When I showed them what we can do for them right now, they said they wanted to be first to sign up!

Position: Once the word gets out, we'll increase our market share and leap ahead of the competition, while increasing our profit by at least 14%.

Acting politically correct with someone who is not/Saying nothing but sounding good! The subject: Nationalism vs. Globalism:

Position: My position on that varies.

Reason: Both nationalism and globalism have merits.

Example: Nationalism can unite an otherwise divided population, especially if it brings people together to overcome a common threat. Yet, globalism helps the world's economies and societies cooperate to bridge gaps and improve quality of life for everyone

Position: So, as I'm sure you can see, one's position on such a vast subject will vary, depending on the specific question asked.

Appendix 3: Suggested solutions to Case Studies in Chapter 6

Case Study 1

After 2 months of dedicated work, including evenings and weekends, you completed an in-depth analysis of your company's product mix. You have identified 3 areas to improve: product pricing, customer segmentation, and vendor selection for raw materials.

Your manager supports your conclusions and arranges for you to present your results in person to the company leadership team. These are people at least 2 levels above you, whom you have never met. At least one of them will resist your recommendations.

Answer these questions as they relate to creating a sense of presence for your presentation:

- What information will you prepare for the meeting?
    - *Lead with the quantifiable improvements, investment required and time before results*
    - *Be able to quickly and simply explain your analysis and why you chose to conduct it*
    - *Try to share the information as a story*
    - *Rehearse, rehearse, rehearse, so you can tell the story without having to think about it!*
- What will you wear?
    - *Choose a classic version of the appropriate attire for your company and your audience's level. Wear clothes that are comfortable and easy to move in. One small 'lucky' or 'confidence' accessory can boost your attitude, too*
- What questions can you anticipate and how will you answer them?
    - *Challenges to your method of analysis and your conclusions*

- What risks or downsides have you identified and how will you mitigate them?
- How have you validated your conclusions?
- Be able to give clear, concise answers! At the end of the question period, use the PREP model to restate your request
- The 'resisting' leader challenges the accuracy of your analysis of product pricing, saying 'you aren't from marketing, what do you know about the marketplace pricing pressure?' How do you answer?
  - Breathe and smile Thank her for her interest and the question. Reply calmly, explaining (briefly) how you checked your analysis and conclusions, and who you asked to challenge them for validity. Best if you can name a respected expert within the company who reviewed and agrees with your analysis

Case Study 2

You own a shirt-making firm in a medium-sized city. A fire at your factory releases thick black smoke into the air, causing the fire department and local government to instruct people to shut their windows and stay indoors. That afternoon, as you are trying to locate all of your employees and contact your insurance company, a reporter from the local TV station arrives with film crew. His first question is 'what toxic chemicals did you have in your plant?'

- How do you respond to his questions?

  o *Be honest, calm and clear. State what you do and do not know. Emphasize that your first priority is the people who work in the factory and the people who live nearby.*

State that you will begin cleanup operations as soon as the experts advise you on how best to do so. Then excuse yourself by saying that you need to focus on dealing with the crisis.

- What should your demeanor (tone of voice, gestures, facial expressions) communicate?
    - *Be serious, calm, and intent. Look the reporter or the camera in the eye. Keep your gestures restrained (waving arms imply being out of control). Try to keep your tone even.*
- After the interview, your assistant asks you the same question. You know that his grandmother lives near the plant, and

that they are very close. How do you respond?

- o *Your demeanor and information are broadly the same, though it is OK to show more emotion with someone you know well. Provide more details, if possible, about the next steps and what he can do to help manage the crisis. Ask if he has reached his grandmother and how she is.*

Case Study 3

You are attending a networking event for your industry, given by a major company in the field. You don't know very many people, but you think this could be a great opportunity to find some customers, or even a new job.

- How do you prepare for the event?

- o *Set a goal (2 maximum) for the event: are you looking for someone in particular, or just to talk with a minimum number of people? Are you looking for specific information? What is it and who can likely give it to you?*
- o *Check whether you know anyone attending and remind yourself of at least one fact about each of them (where you met, what they were doing when you last saw one another, what you spoke about then)*
- What do you wear?
  - o *Clothes that are appropriate for your industry and the location, perhaps one step above what your normally wear to the office.*

- o *Make sure your clothes are comfortable and easy to move in – no stiletto heels or tight belts*
- Do you prepare small talk topics as icebreakers? Which ones?
  - o *Yes! Choose 3 that work for you, and which you can answer easily too*
- One hour into the event, someone you just met, who has obviously spent too much time at the bar, begins following you and insists on joining your conversations. How do you react?
  - o *Take the person aside quickly and explain that you have enjoyed talking with them, but now you have other people you would like to speak with*

- *As a last resort, hide in the bathroom for 10 mins until they find someone else to follow*

Closing thoughts

Did you find this book helpful? You might also enjoy:

- PREP For Success: our workbook giving you more details and plenty of practice with the PREP tool introduced in Chapter 3. Available on Amazon, or at www.fundamentalcapabilities.com or www.steinerinternational.com

- Our professional development workshops and webinars. More information at www.fundamentalcapabilities.com or www.steinerinternational.com

- Coaching from Cindy or Marne. More information at www.steinerinternational.com (Cindy) or www.fundamentalcapabilities.com (Marne)

Your Notes

Use these pages to make your own notes about Professional Presence.

What have you learned?

What are you already doing well?

What do you want to improve, and what steps will you take to do so?